JOHN WALSH
Chopping Wood with T.S. Eliot

salmonpoetry

Published in 2010 by
Salmon Poetry
Cliffs of Moher, County Clare, Ireland
Website: www.salmonpoetry.com
Email: info@salmonpoetry.com

Copyright © John Walsh, 2010

ISBN 978-1-907056-42-0

All rights reserved. No part of this publication may be reproduced or transmitted in any form or by any means, electronic or mechanical, including photography, recording, or any information storage or retrieval system, without permission in writing from the publisher. The book is sold subject to the condition that it shall not, by way of trade or otherwise, be lent, resold or otherwise circulated without the publisher's prior consent in any form of binding or cover other than that in which it is published and without a similar condition, including this condition, being imposed on the subsequent purchaser.

Cover artwork: *Annual Rings* © *Tilltibet* | *Dreamstime.com*
Axe image: *Lisa Frank*
Cover design & typesetting: *Siobhán Hutson*
Printed in England by imprint*digital*.net

To Johnny and Pearl, in memory

Acknowledgements

Thanks to the editors of the following publications where some of these poems first appeared:

Acumen, Crannóg, Cyphers, Ouroboros Review, Poetry Salzburg Review, Revival, ROPES and *Southword*.

Thanks also to my poet friends in Galway who workshopped many of these poems with me. Many thanks to Jessie Lendennie for taking me on-board Salmon, to Siobhán Hutson for keeping me afloat and to Lisa Frank for the axe and sundry bits and pieces.

Contents

From My Blog	13
Downturn	14
Chopping Wood with T.S. Eliot	15
Interlock	16
Del Pinto	17
Making-Do	19
Potsdamer Platz, sometime	20
Under Repair	21
Buzzards over Barcelona	22
Big Blue Towel	23
Direct Debit	24
Reality Check	25
Mámean	29
First Stones	31
The Road to Damascus	32
Silt	33
Island Lights	34
Summer House	35
At Vauvenargues	36
The Creamy Biscuit Man (Reprise)	37
Indreabhán	38
Sea Spinach	39
Incriminating Evidence	43
Silent Witness	44
The phone rings	45
Oregon	46
Special Powers	47
Racket	48
Yes, Minister	49
Tipping Point	50

At the red walls	53
'The Watchmaker'	54
Red Hugh or the Flower of Youth	55
Accidents	56
The Pass	58
Hindsight	61
One of Us	62
Burntollet	63
Spread-Eagle	64
Green	67
Five Vignettes	69
Last Minute	71
Talk Shop	72
The Two of Us	73
There and Then	74
A Break in the Clouds	75
Igor	76
Hare	77
Check-In	81
Tranquillity	82
On finding 'Johnny tell Them'	83
Word of Mouth	84
Cutbacks at Merlin Park	85
Minus Broadband	86
Claims	87
Milchstrasse Number One	88
Things you remember on a Saturday	89
Sales Pitch	90
Adoption	91
Finally	92
About the author	95

Harvesters

Men with tractors cutting lines,
contented when the fields are shorn;
combing bales in perfect weather,
leaving stubble trails behind.

From My Blog

Monday evening read in Cork in The Long Valley.
To seventeen people. Didn't use the mike because
I had a sore throat. Not sure my audience got it.
Told myself I'm not Tommy Tiernan.

Billy Ramsell was there, looking a bit lost
without Neil. Well, that's what I thought.

Wondered what exactly the other one hundred
and ninety-thousand, nine hundred and eighty-three
people in Cork were doing.

There was nothing on except Charlie Bird.

The waitress in Zaks told us they had a busy weekend.
She was glad of the chance to catch up on things.
I felt like telling her I didn't have her problem.
First time I had kangaroo.

This morning dropped into Waterstone's, had a peek
at the new Heaney book. The older he gets,
the more he seems to grow on me. Fair play
to him for getting off the fags.

Bought some squid in the English market.
Then headed back to Galway before it got dark.

Works out at twelve and a half cents per mile.
That's at current gas prices. Not counting
the kangaroo. We paid for that ourselves.

Downturn

The new year eases in, sizes us up clinically.
House prices are falling, construction workers
come full circle with reality. The taxi-driver

predicts a slow year. A cigarette cupped in his limp hand,
he laments the hike in diesel and the flight to London
he had to pass on. A hundred euro down the drain.
It was a busy Christmas for him, no time for a break.

Near Loughrea a rainbow etched into the sky drags
down onto a handful of trees, then scrolls eastward
to take in some farmhouses. The low fields are littered
with listless pools. The storms that battered Donegal

just missed us. We scrape from January what we can,
take cold comfort in its moodiness. A greyness,
clinging to the breeze, settles with uncanny ease.

Chopping Wood with T.S. Eliot

This Eliot guy is really pushing it. Just pulled
his Polonius stunt on me again. Since he
got back from his trip to Paris, he's lost
the plot; he only has been acting strange.

I don't know. He better not get too close
to my axe. Keep his pilfering fingers to himself.
I've got to get all these dead trees chopped up
before the rain comes, with or without his help.

You can't let guys like him walk all over you.
Damn it! The language is as much my birthright
as it is his. His cups of tea and endless questions
get up my nose. This has really gone beyond a joke.

Any murdering around here will be done on my terms.
And all this disturbing the universe can be put on hold
until we get this wood stacked dry before the rain comes.
It won't burn a damn if it gets soaked.

Interlock

Maria D'Antuono, ninety-eight years old, who
was trapped beneath the ruins of her house after
the earthquake in L'Aquila, told reporters she had spent
the thirty hours, while she waited to be rescued, knitting.

When they carried this skinny, little lady out, a ghost
from the dust and rubble raised on high, she smiled
for the world press and mimed with shaky hands
two needles clicking.

                    Since then I have decided
to take up knitting. When they carry me out after
my trauma in the ruins, I will have my handknit Aran
sweater mended, the one my girlfriend always borrows.
My hair matted, contrite with quake ash, I will brave
the international media to show I am a survivor,
following in the tradition of Signora D'Antuono.

Del Pinto

For me he was only a name
but my sister says she'd
heard of him also. He was
something my father held onto,
a dream for another lifetime,
not this one.

I think my father prayed for him
at night on his knees,
bent over the settee,
his back to the dying fire.

I imagine he thought of him at times
when his heart wasn't in the job;
allowed himself a fleeting visit
from an old friend who was part of him,
the way other things weren't.

Maybe he was my father's Kerouac,
the alter ego of a man
who never touched a drink,
who put his wife and family
before everything, and himself
too far down life's scale to ever
stand a chance of making that trip,
of hitting the road or working his passage
on that ship, the way Del Pinto did.

My father was three years older than Kerouac.
He cursed when a watch spring broke,
mumbled under his breath when my mother
got on his nerves. He told me Kerouac was a bum.
No real man would rat on his friends,
name names just to sell a book.

Del Pinto was above all that.
My father's prayers brought him
safely to whatever harbour his ship docked,
where he drank whiskey highballs
behind my father's back, just like Jack.

Making-Do

I think we need a new nail brush. The one on the bathroom rack looks pretty sad. I won't even try to guess its age.

The problem is I'm one of those people who like to hold onto things way past their use-by date. The you-never-know-when-it-could-come-in-handy mindset. Like my father and my grandfather and I suppose all the other fathers down the line, right back to when we were simple cavemen and the local stores closed at six in the evening sharp.

My father had boxes and tins for washers and watch parts. Though when he went looking for something, we all knew what that meant. He would lose his temper, curse and fume. Normally he was a patient man.

He had his first heart attack when he was fifty-two in their Dublin hotel on the night before I got my degree. My graduation photo shows my mother and me side by side in the big hall in Earlsfort Terrace, forcing stony-faced smiles. My father was in the Mater, fighting for his life.

I thought of him often when I was in Germany. After the Wall came down, I got the chance to go East before things changed. I felt at home there. Everybody was used to saving things, sharing and making-do. With all his ways, my father would have felt at home there too.

Potsdamer Platz, sometime

Gisela asks me to make the ride with her.
It's a nightmare alone. There's a guy in Berlin.
She ends up marrying him, but not for long.

It is a ride into the landscape of nihilism,
the mindset of *verboten*,
the void of virtual transit.

'No matter what happens, don't stop,'
Gisela warns me as the headlights flail
against the night.

The Wall is an afterthought,
a cryptic reminder of where it is not at.
They wait two months after I leave,
then knock it.

These days I make breaches of my own,
hammer and chisel tempo, close to the bone.
Potsdamer Platz. 'Don't stop, John!'
Gisela tells me.

I'm on the right track. She's been there.
Sometimes you end up undoing the done.

Under Repair

We come up out of the Underground,
hoping for a romantic moment.

But they've turned off the fountain,
put up a steel fence and a notice
that says: 'Repairs in progress.
Visitors are requested not to proceed
beyond this point.' It reminds me

of our plumber trying to locate the leak
in our en-suite shower. Every day for a whole week
he would arrive with his music box, blast it out,
force us to listen to Willie Nelson. All day long.

Our lives are too precious for that kind of carry-on.
I swore never to let another workman into the house.

But Trafalgar Square is a different kettle of fish.

Buzzards over Barcelona

Who says you can't see them?
They are right there above us
on the Placa Reial, where two lovers
embrace longer than is humanly possible,
making me feel left out of it.

Ominous looking creatures, hovering
on some mission. Whatever attracted them,
they're not for backing off.

I was ready to leave but persuaded myself
to catch some last sun. Who knows when
I'll get the chance again.

Then
the street cleaners in their BC Neta tuxedos,
fluorescent bow-ties and white dandy gloves
turned up. Instantly
captured everyone's attention.
Put on quite a show.

Two flamenco guitars strumming
from under the arches of the cerveseria.
Even the Coca Cola guys selling anything-but
decided to take a break.

Those buzzards just kept hanging there,
right where they are now.

Big Blue Towel

This big blue towel is mine.
I never had as big a towel before.
My sister-in-law, who gave it to me,
always gives me very useful presents.

I can wrap myself in it, snuggle
into its soft touch and reminisce
on my childhood, when I never
had my own towel like this.
As if it were the only thing
I ever wanted to have.

But there were other things I had.
My flashy red sports car that I sat into
and pedalled down the street under
the noses of the other kids who all
wanted one just like it. My green
racer, the latest Raleigh, that I sailed
to school on and back, feeling elite.
Probably things too I don't remember.

You know when I think back on it,
I really didn't do too badly.

However, my therapist gets me to drag up
all kinds of things that might not even be there.
He says when I dig down deep enough,
that is the way I will pull myself out of it.

I'm not so sure. He might just be jealous
of my big blue towel. I'm pretty certain
he doesn't own one. He's got a wife and
six kids, two of them going through college.
Lives right in the middle of town, near a busy
roundabout. I think he could use a holiday.
I'd be alright till he gets back. I'd just
take lots more showers until he does.

Direct Debit

November is not such a great month for me.
For some reason paranormal things begin to happen.
I mean, I seem to get more telephone survey calls

in November than in any other month. Or the line
goes dead and Eircom tell me they cannot trace
the fault. Maybe my neighbour doesn't pay his bills.
Then middle of the night the phone comes back on,

bang into my dream. A familiar voice inquires
if everything's alright now. I think it's my therapist
and start my *spiel* about how from here on in
every day is a bonus. When he hangs up on me,

I make a mental note to cancel his direct debit.
I believe in miracles but this is like pushing it.

Reality Check

At any given moment we could be washed away by a massive tidal wave sweeping in from the bay. An Irish tsunami with our names on it. Afterwards we would be so many bodies, bloated beyond recognition, irrelevant statistics that don't bear thinking about.

We would be a thirty-second news item, a picture or a headline vying for the attention of people too busy to care. Most people, I'm pretty sure, would simply go on making coffee, simmering in tailbacks on the M50 or packing three-for-twos into cutprice Tesco trolleys. But not us.

We would be gone. Maybe a few people might stop and think and realize that at any given moment a massive tidal wave could sweep in.

Máméan

Fair play to you.
You knocked the anger out of yourself,
scorched the earth within you, rolled your tongue
around the curse of your existence.
Look where you are now.
Whipping your poor donkey up that steep mountain
to get out of the wind and rain. You're a sorry sight
to a world that doesn't give a damn. No pity
for your plight, no interest in you whatsoever.
Not a soul among us would change places with you.
But fair play to yourself.

From the half-light the passing souls torment you,
to see how far they can push you. If you
were left alone, you'd maybe hold out.
But they have no hearts.
The wind guts your candle.
In the dark they break your patience,
head off your swipes at their mockery.

I'll make my way up one of these days,
to see if you are still there. These winds
are too fretful for me. And that road.
There's money to be got out of them this year
for that devil of a road. After all their talk.
How can you stand it when not a being
darkens your door? Fair play all the same.
Fair play to you.

There was nothing but the leaden light
weighing down the horizon,
the stripped stacks of the mountains
bowed in going nowhere. They saw
some terror in their day. No two ways.

I warned them not to cry,
but with your body and the life
gone out of it, there wasn't a hope.

Where to? What difference does it make?
To whatever is out there waiting to recall.

If in the end we are all there, I said,
and you're not, what good will there be in it?
What if none of us are there, I said?
All the good will be taken out of it.
But if there is no end, it will be all good.

The donkey waits by the darkened lake,
hugs the lee of the mountain, hungry
for a trickle of sun to fall on its path.

First Stones

I am a relative stranger in these parts
where the dogs leave little for the picking.
You are a grey people. Could it be
the lack of sun that has you this way?
All sweaty and panting, you think
you have run the course. Nothing
could be further from the truth.

When your women step out of line,
you would turn on them, if you thought
you could get away with it. Thank god,
those days are gone. They'd soon
go for you if you tried that one on,
leave you with the long nights
to bring you to your senses.

What goes on behind closed doors
is no one's business anyway.
There are no first stones
worth talking about any more.
When it comes down to it,
we are all suspects.
It seems to be our fate.

Sometimes we need to lick our wounds,
take a chance and lower our defences.
But around here
a place for that is hard to come by.

The Road to Damascus

No, this is not Damascus.
This cold hoof print in scaly rock
is nature's jest, these irate trees
a sparse token. Follow this road.
From where it ends, it's a stone's throw.

This is not Damascus.
There is little to uncover here.
On the pier visitors flick pennies
into the waves, get the local lads to fetch.
They look upon it as a game,
while we stand there and do not object.

The sky here plays tricks.
The last wild geese in moody sequence
confused our thoughts. We watched
them veer off into indifference,
leave us with a premonition.

We have our share of passers-through
who tire us with their constant questions.
Their resolve is hard to doubt.
But there is little we can do.
We have nothing new to offer.

No, this is not Damascus.
Here we go about our business,
reluctant to cause offence.
We've learned to live with the attention.
The road continues past the trees.
This place is hardly ever mentioned.

Silt

Relentlessly the waves surge
into the rock pools of our lives,
stripping our defences,
twist and turn upon themselves,
lashing shapes out of crusted bark.

Between the headland and horizon
it is a stone's throw. Eight geese
strike east, chanting in chorus.

If I could drag down the sky I would,
scratch out its eyes
with sea-fingers boned sharp
from clawing the shingle.

Wind-taunted the ocean rages,
rattles a mophead of curls.

We have been dredged through the depths,
washed up here, gathering the hurts
under each contrary rock, salvaging
morsels in an aftermath of self.

(In this sand and sediment
our most hidden fears are layered,
shreds of ourselves smothered
under salty ash.)

A man swinging a white bucket would make more sense,
selling for a pittance what little he has scavenged.

A hush of wings to the islands crosses,
a silver ripple shivers.

Where are the ones who will dig out the ancient spells,
bury the tattered relics beneath the winds?

Island Lights

The island lights fool nobody.
There is no point in going there.
At this time of night it is distance
that makes them seem inviting.

Once off the island, it is rare
to go back. You're better off anyway
sticking it out in any given city,
even on your own.

Outsiders have been known
to want to prove us wrong.
We give them a wide berth.
Let them get on with it. One day
they can take it no longer.

We've more now than we ever had. Still,
it is hard not to cling to our old ways, like
hens in the backyard scraping and picking.

Something inside of us just won't let go.

Summer House

That man felled trees on the border of our holding.
Within his rights, he left these crippled stumps.
The sun they stole from him cuts into our hearts.

There is anger in the simmering of the season,
bitter in the tangling of the roots.

When the time is right, we will move closer to the lake.
Sometimes we swim across and back.
You see that house? It stands alone.
It cannot be reached by road.
They ferry everything from the lower bank.

The wind unhinges the hanging blossoms,
makes them scuttle across the lake.
Today the water reads twelve degrees.

There is anger in the lapping at the edge,
bitter in the scouring of the rock.

We will forge our own place again. In the evenings
pike will stab the air, gasp at phantom flies,
the voices of our children mirror off the lake.
We will save the birch for one year before firing.

There is anger in the stillness of the land.

At Vauvenargues

Picasso hadn't said a word. Not that he had to.
Just listened to me rambling on. Made me
feel at ease, even though I didn't know
if his English was up to it.

Later in the grounds of the chateau,
he told me Breker probably had saved him
from the Arbeitslager. In forty-three. Not
many people knew. He seldom mentioned it.

I felt that I had wasted his time,
raking over all my incessant doubts.

As I was about to leave, he touched my shoulder.
'Today we are here to make our mark,' he said.
'Tomorrow has not yet touched the horizon.'

The Creamy Biscuit Man (Reprise)

Trousers hanging from his skinny arse, he fumbles
in his pocket for cash. I don't want his money,
I try to tell him. The last poem was more than
worth my trouble. But he ignores me, stuffs euros
into my hands. Then clutching a Feeney's butchers' bag,
he steps out into the road in front of passing cars.

Another drink in Hughes' is all he wants now.
And in the end the taxi money will be forfeited.
How he makes it home he won't remember;
sometimes the brother, who drives the SUV,
the one who got the mother's house, will find him.

It's a year since I first met the creamy biscuit man,
talked shop as we drove past Silver Strand. And
nothing has changed, he hasn't changed a bit.

Indreabhán

This beach is clear now, ready again for wrecking.
Waves rally around the rocks, reclaim lost ground.
A fishing boat idles out of context near Inis Oírr.
A sailing boat skims Blackhead,

passes cursor-like across the Burren.
Those Burren eyesores, nothing
has moved on them since I came here.

At the pier a van drives up,
two figures check on moorings,
then disappear.

There is nothing special to report.
The wind repeats itself, gears up in defiance.
The clouds are locked in an alliance,
a solid web of grey drifts in.

Sea Spinach

Wind from the east, the clouds curl at the ends.
A local fisherman checks on his curragh,
his green ex-post van stands out on the pier.
Another new house going up, its skeleton
roof gleams in the distance.

The sea spinach is thriving, after winter rains
and early sun flourishes like weeds,
a velvet coating thick on the leaves.

Gerry says throw it in the pan
with a pinch of butter and some nuts.
A few minutes will bring out its tangy taste.

The brown foal sprawls on the coarse grass.
Its mother, pestered by defiant flies, is
cautious at first, then tugs at the long stems.

Incriminating Evidence

Poetry doesn't cut it on the streets. Fear has been injected into the veins of people who will never read a poem. A death can be arranged for less than the cost of a print-run. A free call from a mobile phone will get it done. A call from someone whose hands remain unsoiled, to whom poetry means nothing, to whom life and death are just flipsides of a coin.

Poetry loses relevance in the context of the six-one news, on which a young killer hoodie is hustled into a courtroom before a judge who is under no illusions about his powers. He will send the accused to Wheatfield where his mates run the show. The man who made the call is right there by his side. The message is clear to those who dare to get involved. Poetry will not protect you, the judge's hands are tied.

Poetry brings no comfort to the relatives of the dead. Nothing could be further from their minds while they stand by the grave. Nothing can replace what they have lost. Each one must decide, was it worth the price? Poetry can be observed among the mourners, ready to offer a hand in sympathy before it walks away; there is a point at which it turns around to take in the whole scene. Poetry can not think of anything to say.

Silent Witness

All night the bushes wept,
the shameless ground denied its part;
a button missing on a coat
tells more than any other truth.

No one was heard,
no one was seen
in how little time
it takes between.

And where is truth,
and what comes after,
under the leaves,
under the torn?

And how will the night
the silent witness
hold back its anger,
hold back the dawn?

(In memory of Manuela Riedo)

The phone rings

and a voice tells you,
'Your home is on our bombing list.'

Do you think how nice of them
to let you know and pack up and go?

Your neighbour's child playing
in the street is decapitated
by a missile fired from a drone.

Does it make you want to stop and think?

Or should we simply
switch channels, watch
Pat Kenny do his Late Show
thing? Accept the version of
the groomed officials
who stalk our screens,
who claim this is
a retaliatory strike
in self-defence?

Only
the figures do not add up.

For all the tunnels dug,
all the rockets fired
from this disfigured land,
this is no just war,
there is no just cause.

What do we do?

When your phone rings
and you are told it's time
for you to go, there is
no other channel,
no Late Late Show.

Oregon

The police officer said it was his duty to pump five rounds plus into the barefoot young man who was seen acting suspiciously.

Within hours he was an international news item, another trigger-happy cop on administrative leave.

Three days later there is still no weapon, no statement from the deceased.

His family wait for the cover-up, for the press release to say it was their son's fault, the aggressive manner he knocked on someone's door, the violent way he crumpled to his knees.

A neighbour had alerted the cops to something out of the ordinary. It's a quiet suburb where people like to breathe freely.

Special Powers

I remember in '75 the Sergeant
came to the house, asking questions
about a hold-up.

       He said they were doing routine,
door-to-door check-ups to find out if people
had noticed anything. And by the way,
was I new in the area? He didn't recall
seeing my face before.

       After he left, I checked the paper
to find out who'd been robbing who. It was
a bit of a trend back then. But there was no
word of any robbery. I found that strange.

       Now
a Chief-Superintendent can give the nod
to bug your house, your car, your workplace
or your bed, if he imagines you have the look
about you, you might be considering
to commit a crime.

       I wouldn't want him to have any idea
what goes on inside my head at any given time.
I don't think I'd stand a chance.

Racket

A judge in Galway hands out a twenty-month sentence
to a foreign national for milking welfare payments
from the state and siphoning diesel from company cars,
to the tune of thirteen thousand, five hundred euro
and some loose change.

                        That works out at six weeks
per thousand, give or take.

                            Into how many lifetimes
does this translate for the siphon experts of the banks
who will never see the inside of a jail?

We watch and wait, while they still do the rounds,
admit there may have been a few mistakes.

You know, I feel lucky not to be a foreign national,
guilty as sin, with a strange sounding name
that does not make for slotting in.

Yes, Minister

While brushing my teeth
I stop to think of the Minister's words
and I feel how lucky we are indeed
to have a Green Minister like him to tell us
not to be wasting water running it
while brushing our teeth.

And I wonder if he's noticed
that it's been pissing the rain for weeks
and the eco-warriors are up to their eyes in muck
in their flooded dugouts on the Hill of Tara.

But he says he is not in a position to go there
for he is afraid of getting his hands dirty
and he'll have to go washing them all over again,
wasting everybody's time and energy,
including his own.

Seamus Heaney thinks it's a disgrace,
but sure nobody listens to him.

Tipping Point

A bird just hit the kitchen window.
A dull thud. Maybe not too hard.

I don't like when this happens. I get
the feeling the energy is wrong.

I go out and check but there's nothing
lying around. Just the cut-off twigs
that I haven't yet cleared away.

Maybe this won't happen for a whole year.
Then within the space of a few days
small birds start straying off course,
nose-diving into these big window panes.

That's what makes it so worrying, so strange.

I feel sorry for them. Maybe I should
put up stickers, the ones you see in libraries,
hospitals and big office blocks.

But I think that would look weird.
This is my home. I live here.

I am the one who planted the trees.
I remember the early years.
Not a thrush, a blackbird to be heard.

Then one day hearing the first notes,
how expectations changed.

So it disquiets when like today
the pattern is broken and something
creeps in to make one think
how finely the balance is poised,
how easily it could tip the other way.

At the red walls

my father punched the local bully
for picking on me. Afterwards he
had to go and apologize to his face.
My mother made him do it, afraid
they might go to the police.

This father-anger seeded in me.
I nursed it like a creed, until one day
I realized it wasn't mine, that I
had accepted it, handed on
from him. I took an axe to it
and cut it down.

But that day
it was important he'd stuck up
for me, gone out on a limb,
even if it meant he lost the head.

'The Watchmaker'

That poem never made it into the school magazine.
One of those first poems, it was needy and bare,
hungry for a scrap of recognition.

For years my father kept it in his wallet.
I saw him unfold and fold it so often, it fell apart.

Poised behind him as he teased a hairspring into place,
breathing in the cleaning fluid fumes we did not know
could do us harm, I mimicked his patience,
his deep-in-thought, unaware how much of him
would leave its trace.

These things became my stock-in-trade.
The hours inside his silent world I have copied,
believing it was of my doing, my own choice.
But now it all makes sense.

What he left unfinished I have taken on,
teasing into place some hairspring thought,
thinking it is mine, knowing it is not.

Red Hugh or the Flower of Youth

　　　He came from the city, from its purgatory
of streets that criss-crossed the heart of its maidenhood,
was raised like the others between the mud and the bare
stone that spawned them. Under the shadow of the
gasyard wall, tobacco spit fouling the dust. And far away
green Donegal, wild with its mountains and its ageless core.

　　　All fibres strewn and spun
in the messianic factories, where the young girls
turning woman laboured and learnt the apron lore,
their steady feet tramping and turning.

　　　All part of, he was taught their hard love
stained with blood. As if out of the sodden land
kings would go forth to wind-gutted Aileach.

　　　The flower of youth,
　　　the fog gathering, the rain kissing
　　　the beaten cheeks of Red Hugh
　　　under his weary cowl, waiting.

　　　Gone, like the split second of the sun
　　　　　at the edge of the golden
　　　　　　and the all grey.

　　　Gone, the impenitent and never to be free
　　　　　of the ashes of Doire.

　　　Gone, from the incubate hearts of the factory girls
　　　　　spinning the long yarn in the linen hall
　　　　　　of their kings of shreds and patches.

Accidents

The day my brother went over the bonnet of the car,
a matador over a bulls' horns, smack onto
the concrete, lay wasted
like a discarded doll.

Somebody ran for Doctor Cosgrove while
he was carried in, laid out unconscious on the couch.

Then rushed to Altnagelvin on the back seat
of the car that hit him, the driver still in shock,
repeating he had not been driving fast,
no way had he been driving fast.

My mother threw on something decent,
held his head softly in her lap.
I think that's how it was.

I wrote a poem about it.
Not good enough for you.

Nor the way we talked, not being
politicians', doctors', teachers' sons.
You didn't want us and made sure we knew.

I can still rhyme off
the names of those you didn't want.
Of those who sat there with not a clue what
'Emotion recollected in tranquillity' meant.

Tranquillity, where we came from, was not that big.
Emotion, if that meant feelings, was
the last thing we admitted to.

Recollected?
To this day I have not forgotten any of it.

Nor how when I returned
to be your colleague,
you sidled up to me
to offload your advice:

'Pick the best,' you said. 'There's no way
you can focus on them all.'

You headed back to class
without knowing how your words galled.
How the faces of your chosen few were
brought back in a final curtain call.

Later when I heard the news,
though I knew it wasn't right,
it seemed a kind of justice after all.

The Pass

1

Hard men we come from,
grafted from hard stock.
Men put out to fend for themselves
with not much to go on.

Driven by hard faith
they carved out, marked
every turn.

Not much come and go in them;
not much give and take at all.

That's what we came up against.
All the softening-up did us
more harm than good.

2

The far side of Glenshane
was another world. Since
there was no car for us
to just hop into.

The Derry bus dropped us in Magherafelt,
or near enough, where our cousins' territory
opened up. Back lanes with hay-sheds,

a parlour room left untouched,
an old aunt we'd never heard of,
a lane gate to O'Kane's pub-shop.

3

My uncle had the fingers of a mannequin.
When he played piano in our house,
his car tucked neatly against the kerb outside,
the scent of holy water
dripped from them.

He touched us
with the lightness of his grace,
his aura of exotic places.

The biscuits and the queen cakes on the plate,
the china cup in hand, he sipped his tea
and put his case. My father listened,
drawing on a filter cigarette.

If snow fell
my uncle would not venture on the Pass,
took off early at the very hint of it.

4

'Sweet Heart of Jesus, we
commend our souls to You.'

The prayers rushed in panic
from my father's lips
as our headlights catapulted
against the darkness.

'Forgive us our sins.'

Black ice.

Mocking contrition the car
spun in circles,
shook old faiths to their limits.

No gods about me,
no prayer handy, I waited
for the crash, the onslaught
of a new dimension.

5

We reeled to a standstill, poised
miraculously above the drop.
No crash-barrier. Not an inch
for doubt. My fingers sweating
on the steering wheel.

Off in the distance
Belfast Airport crouched.

Below in the ravine
I heard death chuckle.

6

A few times my father and I
drove back over, for him to stand
under the shield of that lone tree,
mouthing some loss song
to the silence of his brother's grave.

The wind in our ears not answering,
giving us nothing to go on.

Hindsight

'Life's what you make it,' my grandfather used to say,
all smiles as he sauntered out the door to play golf.

In the evenings he played melodeon, sang 'Come-all-yes'.
My grandmother shushed at him when he was rude.

During our summer visits he sat outside on the bench,
his white hair trickling in the breeze; or cross-legged
on the high wall he savoured his pipe,
counting the Swilly depot queues.

On good days he led us through the ragged plantation,
then up over Cnoc na hÁithe,
till we were breathless, hungry, subdued.

When he got the job in Du Pont, he visited
on Saturday afternoons, his baggy white overalls
daubed with decorator's paint; handed out
clove rock and iced-caramel toffees but
was more interested in the sport on Grandstand
than in us. Had his fry before he left to catch the bus.

I sat with him as he drifted into death,
me reaching out into uncertainty, he letting go,
not much older then than I am now.

My grandmother always smiled when he was round her.
That's what I remember.
Still, there are things I will never know.

One of Us

My Aunt Florie had a tongue that could cut you to pieces. The kind of thing families pass on from generation to generation. I have it myself. Sometimes I shudder at the damage it has done.

Florie married an English service-man who after the War became a BBC newsreader. She did her utmost to fit in, ended up sounding more English than him.

For all that she never lost her Tilly's-factory-girl laugh. Just when it seemed she had become one of them, it gave her away. She still was one of us.

The closest I got to my Aunt Florie was the time I visited her in Tunbridge. I remember a sunny afternoon, my aunt ironing my shirts, telling me yarns from her factory days.

Years later at my grandmother's funeral I told her how much that day had meant and said I'd love to come to visit her again. Before I'd finished, she turned on me. 'You'll wait till you are asked,' she hissed.

Being a Walsh, I never did. Then it was too late. They found her body in the hall behind the front door. A neighbour, alerted by the whining cats, called the police. Three or four days she had been dead, they came to the conclusion. Families are such cruel institutions.

Burntollet

I was wearing my fawn duffle-coat from Paddy Bannon's.
The one my mother said made me look like a monk.
It was all about Existentialism anyway but I hadn't
a hope of getting my mother to appreciate this.

There is a picture of me ducking through
the groups of attackers, hooded head tucked down.
Taken from behind, it doesn't capture the non-heroics,
the natural instinct to survive.

        You can not hear the stifled cry
or catch the panic on my face.

I was one of the lucky ones. I made it through.
A good hard whack was swung at me from behind.
He must have been a small man because he missed
my head. The blow thudded into my right shoulder,
muffled by my existentialist cloak.

The RUC man standing beside him caught my look.
Then I bolted on, like some animal beaten
into an open pen or truck.

We left Burntollet, battered and betrayed,
frightened by the curtain that had been raised.

Spread-Eagle

Way before the Troubles ever started, my uncle
Pete insisted you'd get a worse hiding from
a Free State garda than from any RUC man.

When the army raided his house (the time
they raided the whole street) my aunt Josie
swore the officer had been a gentleman.

Yet every week
the Derry Journal carried more pictures
of homes that had been ransacked.

Were people doing it out of spite
to themselves?

Maybe I was glad the night
they pinned me spread-eagle up against the wall,
kicked my legs apart, told me not to make any
funny fuckin' moves or they'd blow my head off.

Green

Green the grass the long the wind
tosses on the hillside fields
yellow the flowers
tumbling waves relishing
relishing what is left
secondhanded on
out of lifes walls
into deaths stone

touch and time
tender and touch not
these gifts these offerings
age stonefingered clasps her neck
i reach out to touch
touch stone

sevens a good number
and three
one nought
one night
we shared
dark forests and stones
hacking ones way
brackenbroken
cut and torn
summer dresses full and long
i saw it felt it
touched and turned it
much and mourned it
the bricabrac
how one gets caught up in it

and what is left
hard to believe
the tide the turn
clean and cut
a knife from an own hand
the shadows that delude
not a sound a whisper a voice echoing

the poets dream is maddening
god help him

a broken track
trodden down the grass
no turn back
a year at the station
the stone under the knee
and bled blood red
how beautiful the passion

now not even that
not even the not that
worked upon like stone
here the cut carefully
there the rough slide
with a touch of humour
the hand deals
let it be said
learn to laugh

this time it is taking longer
an unexpected i say
an unanticipated
turn move a slip up

who would have thought it could so long
the burn the flame the fire the glow

perhaps only perhaps you ask why
why the fuss
because of the what was
the madness
the fairytale delusion

having nothing
remains
desire.

Five Vignettes

There was a moon on the balcony,
where we made love in the dark.
The next day they sent an officer
to say the car had to be moved away.
I thought it was because someone
had got a shock.

...

The smell of bread settles
on the room, smacks
of fullness.

'You left the light on,'
I am about to say. Instead
I draw the curtains,

then ease more turf into the fire;
you scrape black crust from the pan.

In the bay shallow pools
wash dark among the rocks,
winds wrestle with the waves.

...

While you were gone,
three meteors slammed into my life,
the plants sighed and the rocks
closed ranks. Someone's umbrella

drifted down from a passing cloud,
my laundry shivered on the line,
and a new equation evolved.

For a split second the circle
reeled and I realized, it was
all going to happen anyway.

...

Leaving earth
I saw you
waving by the rickety fence.

Even when earth vanished
I saw you.

Then the universe
all aglow
said hello.

...

The clothes pegs on my line
neatly in a row
remind me of my life
not so long ago.

Two magpies in my garden
nibbling the seeds,
remind me of the insignificance
of my basic needs.

The sigh of my estate agent
as he slowly drives away,
reminds me of my soul
on open-house display.

The clothes pegs on my line,
when it's time for me to leave,
will remain where they are
as part of the deal.

Last Minute

This year it's Barcelona. Only you won't be there.
In the days without you, I'll hear your voice,
won't have a clue which building is which.
The Lonely Planet Guide, you say. 'You'll be
stuck for choice.' I suppose there'll be a street café
you used to frequent. Nights the concierge's eyes,
as the slow lift rattles on its hinges. Street noise
from below to which I feign indifference.
I tell myself I'll get through this on my own.
I could have chosen Prague or Rome.

Even if I know you are following my every step,
your feelings crowded in the throbbing streets,
the *mapa turistico* laid out in your thoughts.
On impulse you might regret you have not come.
Had I insisted, you might have given in, your valid reasons
dispelled at a whim. I am certain there will be moments
I'll feel alone, it won't make sense. Still,
I could have chosen Prague or Rome.

Talk Shop

My hairdresser tells me my latest girlfriend is the best one I've had so far. I should make sure I hold on to her. Except for my wife, of course, whom she says I should never have split up with in the first place. But that's the way these things go, isn't it?

Anyway, she's not interested in men anymore herself. We're too much trouble. Always on the mooch. Always wanting the one thing we haven't got. She and her teenage daughter chucked her last partner out. They're doing grand now on their own. Not a bother.

Things are slower alright since the recession took hold. Not so many dinner dances, parties, fewer because-I'm-worth-it treats. People coming in once a month now; before you'd see them nearly every other week. Tips are way down on this time last year. The Celtic Tiger has a lot to answer for. Had to be a male, just had to be, she insists as the scissors click suspiciously.

She'd love to go off to India again for a couple of months. Just pack up and go. But when you're running your own business, you have to think twice about doing these things. People are very fickle. She'd probably end up losing half her trade, pure jealousy because she upped and went.

Anyway, we're all done now. Is that alright? Not too short? She knows I never like her to take too much off but you have to give your hair room to breathe. Don't forget now to use a good conditioner and make sure to hold on to that new girlfriend of mine. She's got gorgeous hair.

The Two of Us

I lift the chopping board off the table,
thinking to myself 'Why am I doing this?'
but carry it anyway into the kitchen, put it
in a different place.

The look on your face tells me you are
wondering what I'm doing, asking yourself
why the phone rang once and then went dead;

why things that never seemed important before
now suddenly matter; what difference
a door could possibly make, open or shut?

I have the feeling this is bigger
than the two of us. Or let me put it
another way, any meaning this may have
can not be squeezed out of it.

It starts out as quite a normal day.
The smell of coffee, the morning taking time
to shape. When I come down, things seem
okay. Then the phone rings.

There and Then

Last night I dreamt of you.
The me-now dreaming of the then-you.
Eyes averted, you kept your distance.

I remember a softness that was absent.
I remember a mind made-up,
the way your body spoke it.

One of us was leaving, that was clear.
Not clear why, not clear if we should
accept this as the way it had to be.

Nor as it has to be now.

In this dream however neither of us left.
A not-doing stayed us, indecision
held us together.

There

the dream ends. Though
to say it ends is not concise.

In the not-doing there could be no end.
In the not-happening the chance
all has yet to be done.

A Break in the Clouds

The birds have done a right job on our cherry trees. They know when they're on to a good thing. But what about me? How come they don't show no regard for my feelings?

Every last cherry picked clean, miraculous hearts left dangling on shaky stems. I don't get it. These grey August clouds, enough to ruin anybody's mood, ganging up on the bay while the visitors mulch in homicidal rain.

Now that you're gone, I keep repeating I don't need this, I don't need this. Hoping that eventually it will make some sense. I'll settle for a break in the clouds, some peace of mind and a guarantee that one does not have to go through all this again. Not like the cherry trees do, every year.

Igor

The blackbird panics. On my way in
I crossed his flight path. He'll calm down again.
We accommodate each other where we can.

One way or another I have picked up
a few tricks from him. Like his adherence
to routine, his making-ends-meet,
his checking that the coast is clear.
The self-sabotage, I know it well,
when he fools himself into thinking
he has not been seen.

His sense of duty is where I draw the line.
The ritual returning to the nest, a dangling worm
manhandled in his beak. As if this preservation pattern
were in itself unique. I shudder at his self-denial.

With all due respect, I feel he carries it a bit too far.
All this *Le Sacre du Printemps* goes to his head,
when all it really means is mouths to feed.

I'm still struggling to get out of bed,
never mind attending to other people's needs.

Hare

How unusual is it to see a hare
on an uncertain mid-November day
in a barren Connemara field, brown
as a Grecian tan, dark eyes taking in
the world?

Quite unusual I thought as I stopped
to watch it at a distance, probably
visible to it. Not wanting to pose
any threat, I drew the day around me,
took easy breaths.

The hare poised at readiness, cocked one ear,
then whipped around and cleared the sturdy wall.
Darted out of sight.

I would give this some significance but
really it was only a hare I saw
in Connemara on a November day,
unusual as that may be.

Check-In

I have just been given a boarding card for Seat 6D by a check-in machine that refuses to look at me. Its people skills are like zero.

I need to tell it I panic at take-off. I get all sweaty at touch-down. I want the seat beside the blonde-haired girl in the sleeveless t-shirt. I want to have the chance to talk to her, even if I don't get up the nerve. But it doesn't ask.

I don't want an aisle seat where people passing by make me spill my gin and tonic. I might break into an air-rage.

I want to leaf through my in-flight magazine, sneak a look at what the girl beside me reads. That might give me some lead.

But it won't relate.

Next time

I will wait in line for the chance to talk to someone real, like that lady over there with the Julie Andrews' smile, the one who understands me; she will say, 'Have a nice flight!' and surprise me with seat 11B beside the blonde girl because all along she could see it in my eyes.

Tranquillity

Why has that dog stopped barking
in the middle of the night,
just when I was getting used to
the sound of him?

It's not right.
There should be a law against it.

I think he's blind. Never barks
until I get a few steps past him,
after he picks up my scent.

Right now he's freaking me out.
All I can hear is the wind and it reminds me
of this book I'm reading about the moon,
where there is no such thing as wind,
so in reality the flag could not have been blowing
when Neil and Buzz staked it in the lunar dust;
which seems to prove, to some people anyway,
that they never went there in the first place.
Thank you very much.

Wherever that dog has gone,
he's robbing me of sleep. And
that moon doesn't look
like a face to me anymore.

I wonder what Neil sees when he looks up,
being the first man and all. But they say
he's the type wouldn't tell you
in a million light-years.
Well, that's okay, I think.

I only wish that dog would bark.

On finding 'Johnny tell Them' in a Galway Library

All the librarians want is ice-cream.
And to get to the beach. 'We're not
made for heat-waves,' they moan.
Our Irish psyche is genetically linked
to bands of low cloud and rain.
Depression mode.

I'm bursting to tell them, I found my book
in their poetry section, hermetically sealed
in anti-fingerprint plastic. I want to treat them
to candy floss and bumper-car rides. I want to
offer them daytrips to Portrush on the train.

But libraries are such anti-sun places.
No choc ices, no buckets and spades.
They don't even go in for donkey rides.
I'm afraid they'll just be very blasé.

So I don't let on. I just say:
'I'm off to the beach now.
Think I'll have some ice-cream.'
And I walk out real cool with
Sam Beckett under my arm.

Word of Mouth

There's a man dancing at a Paul Muldoon concert
with more energy than the lot of us and he doesn't
give a damn. Wearing shades, he gyrates and whirls.

It's Rock 'n Roll from this Pulitzer guy,
who clutches his Telecaster with Van-the-Man poise.
The drums are heavy, the bass resonates.

Then the lead guitarist breaks a string.

The dancer heckles as Muldoon produces *Quoof*,
'The Seamus Heaney of Rock 'n Roll,' he yells.
Muldoon sizes him up, does not equivocate.
'Heaney is the Seamus Heaney of Rock 'n Roll,' he states.

Four Knocknacarra women, with poised pens, cling to
their *Selected Poems*, wait for their cue. A big noise in
Princeton, this guy's been around, seen a thing or two.

Cutbacks at Merlin Park

The nurses in Physio are dancing An Staicin Eornan.
Five minutes a day, they're having a ball. 'Are
you coming in girls?' the Sister urges. 'Wait
till I get myself a porter,' a big Mayo nurse calls.

'If unattended to, please notify the receptionist,'
a sign on the abandoned counter declares. But would
you chance it? All I want is a pair of crutches. Then

I'm out of here. 'I can't dance,' is a total non-starter,
as all shapes and sizes gallop in closed ranks. Right now,
my hop one, hop two days are numbered, my dirty dancing

has hit a wall. At twelve twenty-five it's business as usual,
bending and wriggling and torture on the rails. 'Don't forget
now, same time again tomorrow, girls. An Staicin Eornan,'
the Sister giggles, then turns to me with a suspicious swirl.

Minus Broadband

I have a feeling my neighbour might know something that I don't know. He's this boat propped up in his backyard for over a week now; has painted it a bright blue, three coats already. I don't think he could get many animals inside though, small ones maybe, one or two.

My neighbour and I aren't real talkers, we just wave to each other from a safe distance. But if I wake up tomorrow morning and he's gone, I'll wonder what it is I've done on him.

I'm used to leading a quiet life. Keep myself mostly to myself. However, if we happen to meet, you can be sure our conversation soon comes round to the broadband thing, because Eircom still refuses to supply it to us, the reason being we live on this side of the road, not on that. It's a real bummer, we tell each other.

Still I wouldn't call that moaning, just acknowledging a kind of truth about our co-existence. But I sure don't like the look of those clouds today either.

Claims

My insurance is forking out two thousand, seven hundred and forty something euro to repair my car. Some idiot ripped the side out of it. 'Whoever did it, knew he hit you.' That's what the young garda in Mill Street, Joe the claims manager and Martin in the body shop said.

It's funny when different people all say the same thing. It gives me the feeling they must know more than I do.

I read on the net that the said insurance company has to pay out millions after the Air France crash. Compensation for two hundred and twenty-eight lost lives, then add on the cost of an Airbus.

'This will be an expensive claim,' some guy called Riley states. So I don't expect them to question my modest bill.

But then
there's the courtesy five day Corsa from the rental company conveniently located right next door. It all adds up.

Same thing happened to me before. Outside the Róisín Dubh some idiot tore the side out of my Galaxy. Whoever he was, he knew he did it.

Docs said he could hammer it out for about two hundred. But I never got around to it. I slapped a Rolling Stones' sticker on it. More people stopped to talk to me about that big red tongue than will ever pass any comment on this now-you-see-it-now-you-don't job.

Because no one will ever know. That what Martin says.

Milchstrasse Number One

I was nineteen when I first arrived in Munich, carrying a suitcase that belonged to one of my uncles. On the spot where I was standing should have been my hotel. It was a vacant lot. I set down my case and tried to think. Strangers passed by. Ireland was far away. I had travelled two days to get here.

I stopped a man and asked where I could find a place to stay. 'Come with me to Lilo's,' he replied in a chewing gum accent. 'Lilo will find room for you.' That's how I came to Milchstrasse. With Portland Bill, to Lilo and Martin's attic flat,

that had three rooms, beds in every inch of space and a cosy kitchen for philosophy and tea. Lilo took me in, made me feel at home among all her other raggle-taggle souls. She found time to listen, then directed me to visit every church, museum and art gallery there was in Munich. I got an overdose of culture in no time. When some guests moved out, a few of us marched with Lilo to Central Station, watched the young people arriving with their backpacks and picked out who we thought would best fit in with us.

End of summer it was my turn to leave, but Milchstrasse had become my second home. I made the trip back as often as I could, helped with the house that Lilo and Martin had planned. The roof was just being bolted into place when the cancer took her.

After Lilo's death, we scattered. There wasn't anyone to announce to us, 'Curly Charlie arrives next week,' waving his scribbled postcard from Barcelona or Rome. No one to press the door-buzzer and wait excitedly, listening to the footsteps. It took time to get from the bottom of the stairs to the top of Number One. We never knew who it was going to be.

Things you remember on a Saturday

I'm trying to remember the name of the couple who lived two floors above us in the house we lived in in Germany. I woke up this morning thinking about this and cannot get it out of my head.

And I wonder if our old landlord, the house painter (like my grandfather, though I never saw that connection before) might still be alive. He always seemed older to us back then, but how much older was he really?

And then there was that white-haired lady living on her own. We knew nothing about her. She would be dead by now for sure. And the grumpy guy next-door with the two pit bulls. The day we moved out he almost looked sad.

'No more Irish music?' he said. All those years he never complained about the fiddle, pipes and bodhrans blasting away into the early hours. The landlord who lived above us not once either.

And I ask myself why all this is going through my head, when instead I should be outside cutting the grass, now that the drizzle has cleared and the sun is out. Then in a flash it comes back to me, they were called Eppe. And I'm amazed at myself, after all these years.

Sales Pitch

The blackberries are early, they look like they're a bit confused. It's barely August and here in Ireland we put up with this mushy rain, mobs of fly-things in the wind-still, lawnmowers going on the blink and mulched blackberries, no good for eating, best left to wither on their stems.

A perfect ocean, the one that spewed and belched all yesterday, now acts subdued, an airbrush image of itself, as if we could be so easily duped.

Why do we expect any different? I ask myself. My memories of Augusts are of steamed-up windows in my grandmother's kitchen, her Stanley range full blast to dry our clothes; tempers frayed, my parents wishing we could pack up and all go home, my father's annual one week's holiday another wash-out.

Fáilte Ireland are to blame with their glossy we've-never-seen-a-day-of-rain and their sunny-south-east brochures. The lying whoors to con us into thinking we are some kind of Mediterranean clone, boosting sales of sun-cream, useless sundecks and chilled Pinot Grigio.

The blackberries are not to blame. They have no way of knowing that our world is out of sync. They just do what is expected of them, stick to their routine. In fact, they might even have grown to like it in the August rain.

Adoption

My sister and her husband have just come back from London with the final bit of paperwork done for their adopted son, Paul. He makes their life easy, smiles at everyone. And even though the whole adoption process cost them a fortune – at least six hundred now for these London flights at short notice – he's worth every penny of it to them. After all the waiting, their world has a whole new meaning.

It is impossible for us to know why things happen the way they do. Though we spend so much of our lives trying to figure this out, we never will.

It's all part of some scheme of things. Or maybe there is no scheme of things at all. It would be nice to think there is someone who has done his homework, worked this out. But if that someone exists, he or she is not for letting us in on it. No way. Then again, that's okay too.

Finally

This is where I am right now in my poetry, writing about the holes in my carpet that needs replacing after the number of people who have walked over it in all these years, each one leaving his own peculiar mark.

When I started out, I was writing about trees, digging up and planting them, sifting clay through awkward towny fingers. Some people were not impressed, no need to mention any names, you all know who.

After that came the relationship phase, where everything including myself fell apart. That's where my therapist comes in. The journey back, the twisted roots, the whole sorry Philip Larkin thing. I think he still lives near that busy roundabout right in the centre of town, my therapist I mean.

Now I write about the small things, quite a lot about what my neighbour gets up to, the one with the boat in his yard. He's interesting. That dog of his must definitely be blind. I could go on and on about the two of them but as you all know, I don't get paid for that.

About the Author

John Walsh was born in Derry in 1950. After sixteen years teaching English in Germany, in 1989 he returned to live in Connemara. His first collection *Johnny tell Them* was published by Guildhall Press (Derry) in October 2006. In 2007 he received a Publication Award from Galway County Council to publish his second collection *Love's Enterprise Zone* (Doire Press, Connemara). His poems have been published in Ireland, the UK and Austria and he has read and performed his poems at events in Ireland, the UK, Germany and Sweden. He is organizer and MC of the successful performance poetry event North Beach Poetry Nights in the Crane Bar, Galway. He has also been known to show up with his guitar and deliver one or two of his own songs. *Chopping Wood with T.S. Eliot* is a collection of sixty new poems to celebrate his reaching the mature age of sixty.